Wolfgang Amadeus Mozart

MISSA BREVIS
in D major

K. 194

VOCAL SCORE

Edited by

RICHARD MAUNDER

MUSIC DEPARTMENT

OXFORD
UNIVERSITY PRESS

OXFORD
UNIVERSITY PRESS

Great Clarendon Street, Oxford OX2 6DP, England
198 Madison Avenue, New York, NY10016, USA

Oxford University Press is a department of the University of Oxford.
It furthers the University's aim of excellence in research, scholarship,
and education by publishing worldwide

Oxford is a registered trade mark of Oxford University Press
in the UK and in certain other countries

9 10

ISBN 0-19-337630-X

Printed in Great Britain

Missa Brevis is scored for S.A.T.B. soloists, S.A.T.B. choir,
bassoon, 3 trombones, 2 violins, double bass,
and continuo (*organo* and *organo ripieno*).

Full scores, vocal scores, and instrumental parts
are available for hire from the publisher's hire library.

Duration: *c.* 16 minutes

CONTENTS

INTRODUCTION

Mozart's autograph score of his *Missa brevis* in D, K.194, is dated 8 August 1774, but the occasion for which it was written is something of a puzzle. The most important festivals at Salzburg Cathedral, at which the Archbishop himself celebrated Mass with much pomp and ceremony, were known as *Festa Pallii*, the next of which (the Assumption of the Blessed Virgin Mary) fell on 15 August. However, trumpets and drums were obligatory at *Festa Pallii*, so their absence from K.194 means that it cannot have been intended for that occasion. The only lesser Cathedral festival at about this time was the Feast of St Laurent on 10 August, but it is scarcely credible that a full set of parts amounting to over two hundred pages of music could have been copied, and proof-read by Mozart and his father, only two days after the autograph was completed. Ernst Hintermaier has put forward the interesting hypothesis that K.194 might instead have been intended for the basilica of St Maria Plain near Salzburg, where a full week of celebrations was held in August 1774, including a Mass on the 19th during which 'the young Mr Mozart played an organ concerto and a violin concerto, to the wonder and astonishment of everyone'. It is, unfortunately, not known for certain whether the Mass or even the concertos were of Mozart's own composition, but the coincidence of dates is certainly suggestive. The concertos could have been K.175 and K.207, both written the previous year.

It is clear from the division of the text into syllables that Mozart (and his copyists) took it for granted that the singers would use the Austro–German style of Latin pronunciation. Apart from the characteristic hard Gs and 'TS' pronunciation of C before AE, E, I, or OE, vowel length in a stressed syllable is determined by whether that syllable is 'open' or 'closed': thus, for example, Mozart's 'prop-ter' in the Gloria has a short O, not the long O implied by the usual modern division 'pro-pter'. Plainsong intonations are obviously expected at the beginnings of the Gloria and Credo. Those included in this edition come from the *Missale Salisburgense* (1605), which remained in use in Salzburg for many years. It includes four versions of 'Gloria in excelsis Deo', but the one labelled 'In Missis beatae Mariae' seems particularly appropriate in view of the date, and the way that the opening soprano phrase in Mozart's setting almost repeats 'in excelsis' from the plainsong.

No distinction is made in this vocal score between the original sources and editorial emendations and additions: for full details, see the full score and accompanying Preface and Critical Commentary, both available for hire from the publisher's hire library. It should be noted that slurs in the vocal parts have been reproduced exactly as in the autograph: Mozart did not use modern-style 'syllabic' slurs. The keyboard reduction has been written with the piano in mind, though it is playable on the organ. Organists should, at their own discretion, add pedals to some left-hand passages, bearing in mind that Mozart's instrumental accompaniment includes double bass as well as bassoon.

RICHARD MAUNDER
Cambridge, 2000

Missa Brevis
K. 194

Edited by
Richard Maunder

W. A. MOZART
(1756–91)

1. Kyrie

Printed in Great Britain

OXFORD UNIVERSITY PRESS, MUSIC DEPARTMENT, GREAT CLARENDON STREET, OXFORD OX2 6DP

2. Gloria

3. Credo

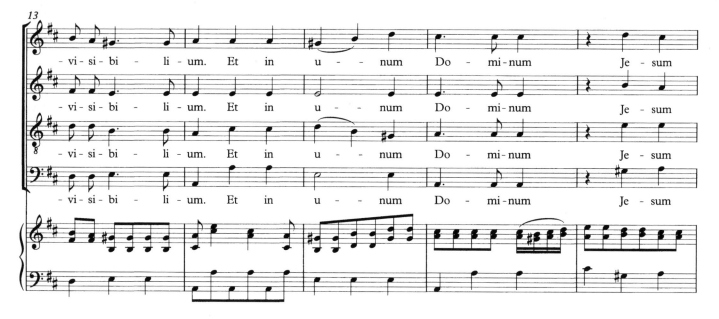

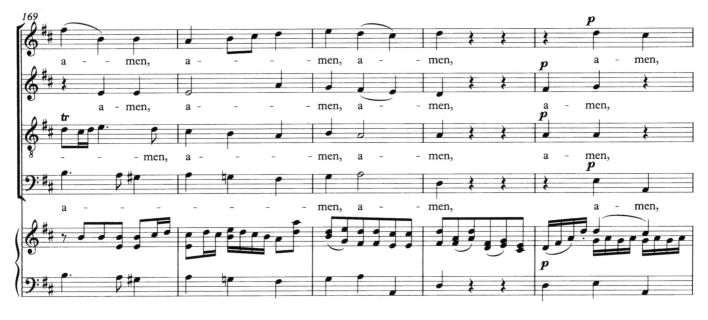

4. Sanctus

5. Benedictus

6. Agnus Dei